Martin Luther King Jr. Day

By David F. Marx

Consultant
Katharine A. Kane, Reading Specialist
Former Language Arts Coordinator
San Diego County Office of Education

Children's Press®
A Division of Grolier Publishing
New York   London   Hong Kong   Sydney
Danbury, Connecticut

Visit Children's Press® on the Internet at:
http://publishing.grolier.com

Designer: Herman Adler Design
Photo Researcher: Caroline Anderson

Library of Congress Cataloging-in-Publication Data

Marx, David F.
    Martin Luther King Jr. Day / by David F. Marx.
      p. cm. — (Rookie read-about holidays)
    Includes index.
    Summary: Presents the history and meaning behind the observance
of Martin Luther King Jr. Day.
    ISBN 0-516-22211-2 (lib. bdg.)   0-516-27177-6 (pbk.)
    1. Martin Luther King Jr. Day—Juvenile literature. 2. King, Martin
Luther, Jr., 1929–1968—Juvenile literature. [1. Martin Luther King Jr. Day.
2. King, Martin Luther, Jr., 1929–1968. 3. Civil rights workers. 4. Clergy.
5. Afro-Americans—Biography. 6. Holidays.] I. Title. II. Series.
E185.97.K5 M3447   2001
323'.092—dc21
                                  00-022638

Martin Luther King Jr.
was an important
African-American leader.

January 2001

Sunday	Monday	Tuesday	Wednesday	Thursday	Friday	Saturday
	1	2	3	4	5	6
7	8	9	10	11	12	13
14	15	16	17	18	19	20
21	22	23	24	25	26	27
28	29	30	31			

We celebrate a holiday
to remember him.

Martin Luther King Jr.
Day comes every year
on the third Monday
in January.

When Martin Luther King Jr. was growing up, there were laws that did not let African-Americans do the same things as white people.

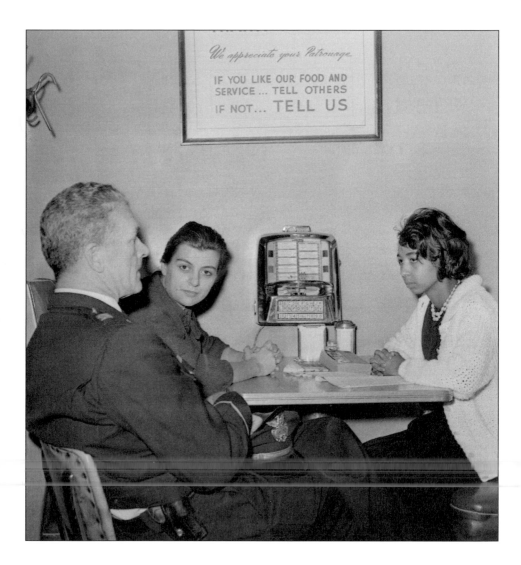

African-Americans could not eat in the same restaurants or use the same water fountains.

Martin knew these laws were wrong. He believed everyone should be treated equally, or fairly.

When Martin grew up, he became a minister. People called him Dr. King.

Dr. King gave speeches. He spoke before huge crowds of people.

He told them that he dreamed of the day when African-Americans would be treated fairly.

Dr. King led people of all colors in marches.

They walked together down highways and city streets.

They wanted the world to hear what they had to say.

Some people hated
Dr. King and the things
he said.

Dr. King was shot and
killed on April 4, 1968.

19

After he died, people
remembered Dr. King
and what he had said.

Many of the laws against
African-Americans
were changed.

Dr. King's wife, Coretta Scott King, tried for many years to create a holiday for her husband.

In 1983, Congress approved the holiday.

In 1986, Martin Luther King Jr. Day was first celebrated across the United States.

Today, many schools and offices are closed on this holiday. People gather together to honor Dr. King.

Martin Luther King Jr. Day can be a sad holiday.

When people remember
someone who was
killed, they often feel
angry and unhappy.

But this holiday can
also be happy.

People feel joy to learn
about the good things
that Dr. King did.

He tried to make the
United States a better
and safer country for
everyone.

Words You Know

Coretta Scott King

Martin Luther King Jr.

laws

marches

minister

speeches

31

Index

About the Author

David F. Marx is an author and editor of children's books.
He resides in the Chicago area.

Photo Credits

Photographs ©: AP/Wide World Photos: 7, 8, 15, 23, 30 bottom, 30 top left, 31 bottom right; Archive Photos: 27 (Tami L. Chappell/Reuters), 26 (John Kuntz/Reuters), 3, 19, 30 top right; Corbis-Bettmann: 11 (Daily Mirror), 12, 31 bottom left (Flip Schulke), 16, 31 top (UPI), 9; The Image Works: 25, 29, (Bob Daemmrich), cover, 20, 24 (Louise Gubb).